بسم الله الرحمن الرحيم

In the name of Allah, the Beneficent, the Merciful

O you who believe, protect yourselves and your families from a Fire
whose fuel is people and stones, over which are appointed angels, harsh and severe.
[*Qur'an 66: 6*]

The Messenger of Allah, peace be upon him and his family, has said:

بَادِرُوا أَوْلاَدَكُمْ بِالْحَدِيثِ قَبْلَ أَنْ يَسْبِقَكُمْ إِلَيْهِمُ الْمُرْجِئَةُ

'Acquaint your children with religious teachings (of Islam)
before the disbelievers get to them.'

'Having children makes you no more a parent than having a piano
makes you a pianist.' Michael Levine

The right of Yousuf Shah to be identified as the Author of the Work
has been asserted by him in accordance with the Copyright,
Designs and Patents Act 1988.

Printed and bound in the UK by
Severn, Bristol Road, Gloucester, GL2 5EU

Published by
Jelly Bean Books
Mackintosh House
136 Newport Road, Cardiff, CF24 1DJ
www.candyjarbooks.co.uk

Dedication

I was born in Pakistan and moved to the UK 15 years ago. I got my first degree in Marketing from Leeds Metropolitan University, and did my master's degree in International Education and Development from the University of Sussex.

I am very passionate about minority and marginalised groups, and this led me to conduct the biggest self-funded study on the transition of orphans in Pakistan, visiting more than 10 orphanages and interviewing more than 80 orphans to find out what happens to those orphans who leave orphanages. My research is available online on various academic websites under the title 'Transition of orphan youth into adulthood in KPK, Pakistan'.

Currently, I am conducting a longitudinal study on Muslims in the UK, interviewing Muslim youth and parents to find out about their youth identities, the root causes of the increasing crime rate and the conflict between Muslim parents and their children. I am intrigued to find out how Muslim youth identify themselves and how they deal with clashes of cultures, languages, and customs. I also focus on those parents who were born outside Europe and raised in a different culture with different parenting styles, to find out if they understand the issues and challenges their children may be facing. There is a big gap between Muslim parents and their children, and I hope to bridge this gap with this book.

I designed this parenting course to help and support those parents who were born outside Europe with little to no education, and those who had conflict in their homes. I interacted with dysfunctional families who were going through a tough time as families, as well as first-time parents who wanted to learn how to bring up their children in a good family environment, teaching children to respect parents and others, manners and hygiene, timekeeping, sharing feelings and the importance of practice their religion, etc. Through teaching, I gained a deeper insight into common issues faced by families; this led to improvement of my method of teaching and resources I was using for my parenting course.

The majority of Muslim brothers and sisters are doing very well, with fantastic businesses and careers, beautiful houses, loving families, and bright futures, but there are also some issues in our community which we should not ignore but rectify. If I can play a small role in this, I will be most lucky and gratified. After extensive research, I have collected some facts and figures below to show how important it is for parents to guide and protect their children from an early age.

This coursebook is designed as a workbook for families to sit together and answer the questions to develop a mutual understanding, recognising the issues both within the family as well as the outside factors that affect them. My objective for this coursebook is that both parents to read through this guide and answer the questions and recognises where and how their parenting style fit into and what more need to be done.

This is a simple workbook based on my experience and hours of research so far Alhamdulillah. I am working on my next edition of this workbook which will be published with more insight details and a comprehensive second edition of this guide InshaaAllah.

Through this book, I hope to bring the whole family onto one page, working one and united. Once understanding develops and communication start within the family all issues and problems can be resolved InshaaAllah.

'A broken family will not make a community; a broken community cannot make a stable state and an unstable state cannot make a solid nation.'

Here I would like to start with some hard facts and issues that Muslim families face in the UK. In the wake of the current Islamophobic environment, there was a 660% surge in Muslims – predominantly teenagers – seeking help with school bullying, depression, substance abuse, and other issues.

Parents report that their children are being exposed to retaliatory anti-Muslim hostility and bullying, in which they are called 'terrorist' and told by their peers in the school playground to 'go blow up another town'.

In 2017 alone, 839 incidents of Islamophobia were reported, amongst which 6% (53 accounts) occurred in educational institutions. These occurrences of Islamophobia-related victimisation in schools highlight the fact that Muslim youth are vulnerable to abuse. They also show that Islamophobia-based bullying is becoming a problem, which in turn increases the risk of young Muslims experiencing difficulties in life and developing mental health problems associated with bullying, such as depression, substance use, and paranoia.

Out of over 2,000 contacts made through Tell MAMA in 2018, 1,282 anti-Muslim or Islamophobic reports were recorded, of which 1,072 were verified through secondary evidential sources.

In 2018, 'Punish a Muslim Day' letters were sent to Muslim homes, institutions, and places of work in March, followed by heightened tensions, fears, and anxieties around the proposed day in April; the second wave of letters ('Punish a Muslim Day 2') was received in May.

The second and more significant spike occurred in August 2018 after the former Foreign Secretary Boris Johnson wrote a column referring to veiled Muslim women as 'letterboxes' and 'bank-robbers'. In the week following his article, anti-Muslim incidents increased by 375% – from eight incidents the previous week to 38 in the following. Of these 38, 22 were directed at visibly Muslim women who wore the face veil (niqab) or other veiling practices. We (Tell MAMA) recorded a total of 57 incidents in the three weeks following the column's publication, 32 of which were directed at visibly Muslim women. Between the 5th and 29th of August, 42% (24) of the street-based (offline) incidents reported to Tell MAMA directly referenced Boris Johnson and/or the language used in his column.

In 2002, 5,502 prisoners in England and Wales said they were Muslim. Three years later, the number had risen to 7,246 and almost a decade on, by December 2014, it had reached 12,225.

Last year (2018), 58% of Muslim prisoners were aged 30 or under, compared with 45% of the overall population, and in what is termed the 'secure youth estate' – institutions which hold 10- to 17-year-olds – almost one in five prisoners was Muslim.

The number of Muslims in prison for drug offences in England and Wales jumped by 63% over seven years, rising from 2,089 in 2010 to 3,406 in 2017, according to figures obtained by The Independent using Freedom of Information laws.

'Mosques and the older generations within Islamic communities don't know how to stop young people turning to dealing, and at a Government level there is no real understanding of the problem,' said Dr Mohammed Qasim, a criminologist at Leeds Beckett University, who has spent more than a decade researching crime in British Muslim communities.

The majority of hate crime offences recorded by police forces in England and Wales were racial: 78,991, increasing by 11% in the past year (2018).

There were 103,379 hate crime offences recorded by the police last year (2018), the majority of which (76%) were race related. More than half (54%) of the hate crimes recorded by the police were for public order offences, a third (36%) involved violence, while 5% were recorded as criminal damage and arson.

The Invisible Generation: We do not see young Muslims in mosques, community meetings, and social occasions. Why?

They are a trapped/suffocated generation, who are bullied and tortured mentally and physically for the colour of their skin and their religion by non-Muslims, while they are belittled, humiliated, and shamed by Muslims for not being 'good Muslims'.

Together we can help and support young Muslims, include them in our society, and make them feel proud of their colour and religion.

Parenting

1.1 Why are you a parent?

What is your concept of a family?

What are the roles and responsibilities of a family member?

Does a mother have to be only a housewife and a full-time mum?

A father is the breadwinner, the absent member of the family. Is this right, and why/not?

How is parenting back home different in Europe? How are children back home different from those in Europe? What are the benefits and complexities of being a parent in Europe?

What is meant by the involvement of both parents, their roles, and the sharing of responsibilities?

What is your family home environment like?

Who is raising your children - mum, dad, or both parents?

How do social media, schools, and society affect your children?

1.2 The roles and responsibilities of being a parent

Our goal as parents is to ensure that our children:

- Feel loved, accepted, and safe
- Enjoy their childhood
- Embrace childhood for what it is
- Are supported when dealing with challenges
- Learn, get an education, and are successful.

In addition to these goals, we also want them to:

- Function in the outside world
- Cope with with negative experiences they may have in life and create positive relationships.
- Make good relationships
- Add value to society.

When children are distressed, upset or anxious, who do they go to, and why?

1.3 Goals as a Muslim parent

We all want our children to:

Be good Muslims and close to our deen.

Have good careers.

Have a good life and their own families.

Contribute to and portray our religion in a positive manner.

The end goal is to have a good life here and in the life hereafter.

As a Muslim parent, what are your goals and expectations for your children and what are you doing to achieve these?

What is your plan for raising your children according to your expectations, or you are making dua for a better future for them every day?

1.4 Your responsibility as a parent

Abu Huraira reported Allah's Messenger (ﷺ) as saying:

No child is born but upon Fitra. He then said. Recite: The nature made by Allah in which He created man, there is no altering of Allah's nature; that is the right religion.' [*Sahih Muslim 2658 d*]

Narrated by `Abdullah bin `Umar:

The Prophet (ﷺ) said, 'Every one of you is a guardian and every one of you is responsible (for his wards). A ruler is a guardian and is responsible (for his subjects); a man is a guardian of his family and responsible (for them); a wife is a guardian of her husband's house and she is responsible (for it), a slave is a guardian of his master's property and is responsible (for that). Beware! All of you are guardians and are responsible (for your wards) [*Sahih al-Bukhari 5188*]

1.5 Dua

When we take all the necessary steps and actions to help and protect our children from the evils of the world and all the harms around us, then we should make dua and ask Allah for help and protection.

Ibn 'Abbas said:

The Prophet (May peace be upon him) used to seek refuge in Allah for al-Hasan and al-husain, saying; I seek refuge for both of you in the perfect words of Allah from every devil and every poisonous thing and from the evil eye which influences. He would then say; your father sought refuge in Allah by them for Ismail and Ishaq (*Sunan Abi Dawud 4737*)

'And those who say, 'Our Lord, grant us from among our wives and offspring comfort to our eyes and make us an example for the righteous.' [*Qur'an: Chapter 25, Verse 74*]

1.6 Children's emotional needs

Acceptance: Accepting our children for who they are, with no comparisons.

How much do you know about your children's life and the emotions they are going through?

Appreciation: How can you raise your children for who they are, their likes, hobbies and interests?

Approval: How can you allow your children to choose their hobbies and pursue their interests?

Comfort: How can you comfort and support your children when they are hurt or feeling 'weird'?

Encouragement and discouragement: Encouragement and discouragement: When your children are doing something positive, how can you help and encourage them to continue? And when they are doing something wrong/harmful how can you divert their attention, mind, and focus on the positive activities, rather than being angry and shouting at them?

Respect: How can you respect your children for who they are, for their opinions and interests? Some parents treat their children like children and expect them to behave like adults. but we should respect our children like adults but expect them to be like children.

Safety and security: How can you let your children know that you are there for them, no matter what happens?

Most Things Our Children Need are Free

2.1 Communication

I am yet to see children ask their parents to buy shares in a bank or business, to buy several properties, or to work every hour of their life, but I have often seen children asking their parents for time and involvement.

From my own experience, I never had a close relationship with my father or had a conversation about my day, feelings and topics I was interested in. My father never talked about his feelings, or involved me in his life. This is the reason I cannot sit with my dad for long periods of time because we have nothing in common and nothing to talk about except everyday chit-chats such as politics or news. As an obedient son, I would like to spend more time with my father and try harder. However, I end up spending more time with my mother, as we are very close, I feel like I can talk to her about anything and everything for as long as possible until she gets tired.

Now, I want to change this behaviour of a "father only being the breadwinner and forbidden from being involved in the children life" attitude. So, I spend time with my own children and try to have more involvements in their life. I believe when we have a good relationship with our children from a young age, that will to build a solid relationship with the parents which will last for life InshaaAllah.

How close are the members of your family?

Do you think you can share and communicate with your family members?

What can you do as a family to communicate more easily, freely, and effectively?

2.2 Health and hygiene

It is important to set routing for our children from a young age such as Sleeping and waking up on time. A healthy child needs certain amounts of sleep depending on their age as well as a good diet to nourish their physical growth. It is also vital to teach our children about personal cleanliness from the young age such as using the toilet, washing hands afterwards, staying clean, washing hands before and after meals etc. Let us give our children good habits: habits are like second nature - they are for life. The importance of good health and hygiene are evident from hadees.

Abu Malik Al-Ash`ari (may Allah be pleased with him) reported that the Messenger of Allah (peace and blessings be upon him) said:

Purity is half of iman (faith).'

A'ishah (may Allah be pleased with her) reported that the Prophet (peace and blessings be upon him) said,

'The miswak (a twig used for tooth brushing) cleanses and purifies the mouth and pleases the Lord.' (An-Nasa'i and Ibn Khuzaimah; authenticated by Al-Albani)

Abu Hurairah (May Allah be pleased with him) reported that the Messenger of Allah (peace and blessings be upon him) said,

'Were it not that I might overburden my followers, I would have commanded them to use the miswak before every prayer.' (Al-Bukhari and Muslim)

How poor hygiene affects learning:

Schools are for social interaction. Poor hygiene can have negative effects on socialising, leaving the children alone with low confidence.

When children lose confidence and feel withdrawn, it affects their motivation and stimulation to learn. It can have a negative effect on their health.

Timekeeping, health and hygiene remain for life and these are the best education we can give our children for free. When we get them to practice brushing their teeth, making their hair, washing and wear clean clothes on with a little reminder. And If these small things are done correctly it will make a huge difference in their life and boost their confidence allowing them to socialise more easily and comfortably.

Let us work on our children's habits, etiquette and greetings. It is absolutely free and we will find out that these are far more important than maths formulas and English literature. Make a timetable and let your children be independent and responsible within the boundaries. Discipline should be used as training rather than punishment.

Here is an amazing quote by Benjamin Franklin:

'Tell me and I will forget
Teach me and I will remember
Involve me and I will learn.'

2.3 Creativity

As we know, parents send their children to school to learn; some of them go on to colleges and universities and almost all of them fight for office jobs. We may agree that all children learn maths, English, reading, writing and all the necessary subjects, but only a small number achieve their dreams and carry on with a happy life, while the majority just work to pay their bills and rent. There are many reasons behind this but the stand-out reason for me is creativity. There is a difference between humans and sheep: humans think differently from each other, while sheep follow each other; unfortunately, if we look around, we see humans acting like sheep and just following one other. All students who take a different route and think differently from the rest of the class tent to be more successful, and this art of being creative is free, regardless of any field or department. You see, there are thousands of careers and businesses, but what happens if someone asks a parent, 'What do you want your children to be?' The answer is mostly, 'Doctor, engineer, accountant, or police officer' and if the children fail to achieve that career, they end up at the checkout in a supermarket or flipping burgers in a fast-food place. If we give our children the Tools to become more creative and intrigue their imagination, they will achieve whatever they want sooner or later and we can stop worrying about their future. Let us find out what our children are good at, what they are interested in and help them pursue it; to do this, we have to spend time with our children. This can be a difficult task as we would rather go out and work, earn money and satisfy ourselves that we have done whatever we could for them. Most of the fathers I meet during this parenting course say the same thing: 'I worked all my life for my children and family, I don't gamble or live a luxurious life, nor do I have expensive hobbies. Whatever I do, I do it for my family and children.' I always ask them the same questions: 'When did your children ask you for a house, car, and a large sum of money in the bank? Were you working day and night to put that money in your children's pockets, or was it your dream and ambition to have a big house, big car, and big bank balance?'

Going back to creativity, I asked myself every day, how can I help my children become more creative? I started spending time with my children and focused on getting to know them better and vice versa. During this process, my son started writing about different topics, he used to write every day, and by the age of seven, he wrote and published his first children's book: 'The boy with Four Super Powers'. I invested my time and money to boost his creativity, confidence, self-esteem, and self-worth. He will be able to use this skill and talent for the rest of his life InshaaAllah

Available Now

Brothers and sisters, we are chasing money and we think money will solve every problem. During this process of earning money and accumulating wealth, our children grow up and stay with us while they need us, but when they become independent and start earning money and no longer need us, we wake up and wish if we could've spent more time with our children. Let us spend some time with our children and get to know them and understand them better. A car is different from a tractor: if we take a nice shiny expensive car into a field, it will always struggle, always, because it Was built for use on the roads, not for fields. If we bring a tractor to the motorway, it will always struggle to keep up with cars, even little cheap cars. We can swear and curse at the tractor but it will still be slower than cars. We can push, slap, or punch this tractor, but it will be slower than cars, because it is not made for roads. Children are exactly like this: they are different and we as parents need to know who they are, their likes and dislikes and their hobbies but unfortunately most parents will only judge their children based on their academic results.

2.4 Confidence

When we see someone, who comes across as outspoken and loud we assume that they are confident; this may not always be the case. Let me give you some examples. If we had to decide between going in a car with someone who is very well-dressed, outspoken and loud and they cannot drive or a quiet, timid person who has 20 years driving experience, who would we choose? Yes, it will make sense to go with a quiet person who has driving experience. If we had a health problem and needed help would we choose to see a medical doctor who is quiet in nature or would we choose a loud, outspoken person without medical profession? We would of course choose the trained medical professional who is quiet.

I want to make the point from these analogies that confidence comes with experience, skills, talent, and practice. If we want to be confident or want our children to be confident, we need to invest our time, energy and resources in them. When they have certain skills, talent, experience, or education, they will become confident, there is no doubt about that. We can teach our children at home to learn about swimming, buy them books about swimming and show them swimming tutorials, but until we physically take them swimming, and teach how to swim, they will never be confident. They may talk about swimming for hours and hours at home and with friends, but when they go near a swimming pool, all their confidence will disappear. We are most confident when we are talking in our mother tongue, as we have practised speaking that language all our life; typically, we will not be very confident speaking another language unless we spend some time learning and practising it.

Do you agree with my theory about confidence? Which parts specifically?

Do you know the strengths, talents, and skills of your children? How are you helping them to polish these skills?

2.5 Truthfulness

While speaking to a parent during my research, he stated that the most important rule of parenting is to be truthful and teach our children to be truthful. No matter what they do, what mistake they make, who they associate themselves with they must learn to always tell the truth when they come home. It makes sense, as when children do something wrong outside, they lie because they are afraid of their parents' reaction. However, if parents do not shout, scream and punish their children and instead explain and solve the situation then their children will always tell the truth as they know that their parents will support them even if they have done something wrong.

We as parents should cultivate truthfulness until it becomes implanted in our soul and our children's souls and dispositions, and it will reflect in our personalities. As the Prophet Muhammad, may the mercy and blessings of God be upon him, related:

'I order you to be truthful, for indeed truthfulness leads to righteousness, and indeed righteousness leads to Paradise. A man continues to be truthful and strives for truthfulness until he is written as a truthful person with God. And beware of falsehood, for indeed falsehood leads to sinning, and indeed sinning leads to the Fire. A man continues to tell lies and strives upon falsehood until he is written as a liar with God.' (Saheeh Muslim)

Prophet Muhammad may the mercy and blessings of God be upon him promised:

'Guarantee for me six things and I will guarantee Paradise for you: tell the truth when you speak, fulfill your promises, be faithful when you are trusted, safeguard your private parts, lower your gaze, and withhold your hands (from harming others).'

Truthfulness is an essential attribute of every single prophet who graced the earth. We are told in the Quran:

'And mention in the Book, Abraham: surely he was a most truthful Prophet.' (Quran 19:41)

'And mention in the Book, Ishmael: surely, he was a man true to his word, and he was a Messenger, a Prophet.' (Quran 19:54)

'And mention in the Book, Enoch: surely he was a most truthful Prophet.' (Quran 19:56)

Parenting Styles

Researchers have studied parents and parenting styles for decades and came up with 3/4/5/6 parenting styles. These parenting style theories are used widely but I am always against "one-size fits all" theories. We all are unique individuals with different cultures, habits, likes and dislikes and this reflects in our parenting styles. I believe parenting should be flexible and adaptable. For example, if you have two or more children you cannot use the same parenting style for all of them as they are all different. One child may be more outgoing and sociable whilst the other may be shy, reserved and an introvert and you have to help and support both of them. If your parenting style is rigid, only one child may get help and support while the other could end up getting neglected unintentionally. For example, with one child you may need to be firm to get them to complete their homework but with your other child you can be gentler and they will still complete their homework. If you believe children are young people with different personalities, tastes, likes and dislikes then you will learn to adapt your parenting style. This is why I believe there are two types of parenting styles: "weak" and "strong" and whatever parenting style works for your children to grow happier and stronger is a "strong" parenting style while whatever parenting style damages your children mentally and physically is a "weak" parenting style.

Parenting Style	Strong and positive parents	Weak and negative parents
Discipline	• Rules are clear • Reasons behind rules • Consistent • Used as training rather punishment	• Strict rules • Inconsistent • No discipline at all • Used as punishment
Communication	• Open communication • Communication without judgment • Clear directions • Clear explanation • Open for negotiations	• No or little communication • Avoid confrontations • One-way communication

Expectations	• Set realistic goals • Involvement of the whole family when setting goals • High expectations with clear strategies to achieve it • Help, support and encouragement to achieve goals • Room for mistakes and revisions	• No expectation • High and unrealistic goals • High expectation without clear directions • No help or support • No room for mistakes
Effects on Children	• Independent • Well behaved • Self-reliant • Socially accepted • Expressive and opinionated • Will know right from wrong • Well balanced life • Happy with family and friends	• Low self-esteem and confidence • Shy and fearful • Socially isolated • Mis-behaves • May suffer from mental health issues • Seek refuge elsewhere from family

them and wish their children were livelier, but if they are lively and active, they try to stop them being lively and active. These parents wish to have a remote control for their children, as when they themselves are happy and in a good mood, their children can be noisy, jumpy, and active, but if they themselves are stressed or tired, they want to mute them. Unfortunately, they fight against their kids' nature until their children hate them and do not want to see or speak to them.

Let us provide a safe, peaceful, loving, and understanding environment at home. Children who do not find these things at home try finding it elsewhere.

3.2 Angry and frustrated parents

The children will be at the receiving end of our anger and frustration - is this just? Frustration is an emotion stemming from challenges and hurdles that stand in the way of goals. These goals might be major and long-term, or minor and short-term. For example, if we are going to a supermarket to get some shopping and there is traffic on the way, it frustrates us but we keep going. When we get to the supermarket and look for parking and we have to wait or go around few times to find a parking spot, it makes us frustrated but we tolerate it and keep going. inside the supermarket there may be queues everywhere which increases our frustration but somehow, we suppress our emotions and go back to the car and go home.

At this point, our frustration level is extremely high and difficult to control; one little thing will make us lose our temper and we will lash out. It might be our partner or our children who do or say something which makes us lash out and take out all our frustration on them - normally it will be our children who are at the receiving end of our frustration. Imagine if we are angry and we have to shout and there are three people in front of us, a policeman, our employer, and our children - who would we most likely shout at? Of course, our children; they are small, weak, dependent on us and they cannot do anything about it; what they will do is keep it in their mind, they will hold on to it until they can do something about it. Usually, these children who get shouted and screamed at by their parents every day cannot wait to leave their house. Even if they stay with their parents, they do not like it. I interviewed several young people who are/were on the wrong path, who admitted they could not bear living at home and when they got an opportunity to get out of their parents' house and earn some money, they grabbed that opportunity, even though it was illegal. I too have a very low frustration tolerance level and when I have to deal with difficult clients, traffic jams, queues for banks and supermarkets, parking and then go home to deal with the limitless energy of my children, I find it very hard to control my emotion. Through the years, I have taught myself not to take out my frustration on my children.

I try to do something to take my mind off the frustration I am feeling, I try to take part in what they are doing and finding an interesting activity for my children and me to do.

The best way I deal with frustration myself is keep saying Astaghfirullah (I seek forgiveness from Allah) which calms me down and at the same time I keep telling myself that I am not special and that everyone is on the road in the same traffic jam or queue, so I should take it easy. When do you find yourself shouting at your children?

Who is mostly at the receiving end of your anger and frustration?

What is your frustration tolerance level? Do you get angry and frustrated very easily or does it take a lot for you to get frustrated and angry?

How do you deal with anger and frustration?

3.3 Handling conflict in a family

Conflicts in families are inevitable and common. How we handle and deal with them is important, the solution can have a positive or negative effects on families, especially children.

Aggressive

They start by shouting and screaming as soon as they see a problem.

They are always right.

They do not want to hear the full story or the other person's side of the story.

The conflicts will become worse until the parents forgive everyone.

Passive

They will not face up to and stand up against something or someone, even when it is wrong and unacceptable.

They hate hassle and confrontations.

"They hope this conflict or problem will go away by itself.

Passive-Aggressive

They pretend they do not care and do not mind anything or anyone when they are wrong, but they actually do and are bothered by it.

"What's wrong? The answer is always 'Nothing'.

They do not tell but actually show with their behaviour if there is a problem or conflict.

Assertive

They remain calm, and communicate clearly and politely when they see a problem or conflict.

They keep themselves and their emotions in control.

They do not shy away from confronting someone if this resolves the issue.

They are willing to listen and understand another person's side of the story.

They are willing to mediate to resolve conflicts.

How do you handle conflicts in your family?

Mental Health

Mental health includes our emotional, psychological and social well-being; It is important because it affects our behaviour, thoughts and how we feel. Mental health determines how we manage our relationships, how we deal with stress, pressure and most importantly how we perceive ourselves. The National Institute of Mental Health sums up mental health perfectly with its slogan "No health without mental health". It is a complex subject and I will highlight the key symptoms but if you are concerned about your or your children's mental health, I have listed some organisations below who offer free help and advice for mental health.

Negative view of myself	Anger attacks
Feeling tired all the time	Withdrawal from social activities
Low self -esteem	Guilt
Indecisiveness	Neglecting hobbies
Lack of trust	Isolation

Avoiding contact with friends

Negative view of the world

Feeling worthless

Lack of motivation

Lack of interest

4.1 Anxiety

Anxiety is what we feel when we are worried, tense or afraid. These feelings are normal and everyone has them when they are at a job interview, before an exam or meeting new people. However, these feelings might be constant and affect our performance, body language, and thoughts on a daily basis - particularly when thinking about the future. Anxiety becomes a problem when we are concerned about self-perception and constantly think about it and we avoid socialising (body dysmorphic disorder (BDD) creates social anxiety). How do you know if your children are distressed or anxious?

What do you do when your children are distressed, unhappy or anxious?

What do you do when your children are distressed, unhappy, or anxious?

4.2 Depression

Depression is more than simply feeling unhappy or fed up for a few days.

Most people go through periods of feeling down but when we are depressed, we feel persistently down for weeks or months, rather than just days.

Depression has a stigma attached to it and most people, especially children, will not accept that they are suffering from depression (whether it is mild or severe).

What do you know about depression?

What do you know about the help and support available for depression?

Does it hurt your ego and pride to accept you are suffering from mental health problems? These issues can be minor, mild or severe.

When you are facing hardships turn to Allah.

For all Muslims who are sad, anxious or depressed they should remember the year of sorrow when Prophet Muhammad lost his uncle Abu Talib who was his protector and ally, and his beloved wife Khadijah (ra). Furthermore, he was ridiculed, rejected and stoned until he was bleeding when he travelled to Taif. This was the time of sadness, grief and suffering for Prophet Muhammad and his companions but Allah gave him a truly amazing, beautiful and comforting gift of Salah on the night of Miraj. This is when Allah told Prophet Muhammad and indeed all the Muslims 'with every hardship [there will be] ease' (Surah 94).

Focus on Salah and Dua:

Whenever we are sad and facing difficulty it is very important, we turn to Allah and pray properly. Our teacher used to say turn your practice "up and down, kiss the ground and back to town" into prayer. Focus and extend your prayers, take your time and imagine Allah is watching you.

When we make dua, we should beg Allah with persistence to help us in the time of difficulty and hardships. . Imagine if a beggar was begging for money whilst running, he was not stopping or being persistent, is he likely to get money from anyone? He most likely won't because he is not taking his time to stop, ask for money and explain the reasons. Us Muslims pray and make dua like it's part of our routine, we do not take time to ask Allah sincerely and with persistence believing it is only Allah who can help us through the hardships and difficulty.

Dua for Anxiety and Depression:

Prophet Muhammad used to make this dua to Allah every morning and evening.

اللّهُمَّ إِنِّي أَعوذُ بِكَ مِنَ الهَمِّ وَ الْحُزْنِ، والعَجْزِ والكَسَلِ والبُخْلِ والجُبْنِ، وضَلْعِ الدَّيْنِ وغَلَبَةِ الرِّجال

'O Allah, I seek refuge in you from grief and sadness, from weakness and from laziness, from miserliness and from cowardice, from being overcome by debt and overpowered by men (*Al-Bukhari: 2893, 5425, 6363, 6369*)

اللَّهُمَّ أَصْلِحْ لِي دِينِي الَّذِي هُوَ عِصْمَةُ أَمْرِي، وأَصْلِحْ لِي دُنْيَايَ الَّتِي فِيها مَعَاشِي، وَأَصْلِحْ لِي آخِرَتِي الَّتِي فِيها مَعَادِي، واجْعَلِ الْحَيَاةَ زِيَادَةً لِي فِي كُلِّ خَيْرٍ، وَاجْعَلِ الْمَوْتَ رَاحَةً لِي مِنْ كُلِّ شَرٍّ.

"O Allah! Set right for me my religion, which is the safeguard of my affairs. And set right for me the affairs of the world wherein is my living. Decree the Hereafter to be good for me. And make this life, for me, (a source) of abundance for every good and make my death (a source) of comfort to me and protection against every evil."[*Muslim, 2820*]

اللَّهُمَّ إِنِّي أعوذُ بِكَ مِن جَهْدِ الْبَلَاءِ، وَدَرْكِ الشَّقَاءِ، وَسُوءِ الْقَضَاءِ، وَشَمَاتَةِ الأَعْدَاءِ

Oh the Allah, I seek refuge in You from the distress of trial, from the lowest level of misery, from the perversity of fate, and from the malicious rejoicing of enemies. [*Bukhari and Muslim*]

اللّٰهُمَّ رَحْمَتَكَ أَرْجوفلا تَكِلْني إلى نَفْسي طَرْفَةَ عَيْن، وَأَصْلِحْ لي شَأْني كُلَّه لا إِلَهَ إِلَّا أَنْت

O Allah, I hope for Your mercy. Do not leave me to myself even for the blinking of an eye. Correct all of my affairs for me. There is none worthy of worship but You. [*Ibn Hibban, 864*]

4.3 Low self-esteem

Self-esteem is the opinion we have of ourselves. We all go through periods of time when we lack confidence and do not feel good about ourselves.

But when low self-esteem becomes a long-term problem, it can have a harmful effect on our mental health and our lives.

Living with low self-esteem can harm our mental health, leading to problems like depression and anxiety.

Some parents unconsciously compare their children with others and tend to tell them, 'Look, your friends are doing so well, they are ahead of you, they are cleverer than you, they are achieving more than you.' These children eventually accept that they are not good enough, they are less intelligent than their friends and they create a low image of themselves in their own mind.

I have four healthy children; sometimes I find it difficult when they jump, scream, and shout all the time with limitless energy, but I am ever so grateful to Allah for giving me healthy and active children. My whole mindset changed about my children when I worked with special needs children: I will never forget the happiness on their parents' faces when their children just said 'Hello' or 'Bye' to them. I realised what a great gift it is when we have able-bodied children who are healthy and active.

In what ways do you compare your children with others?

How happy are you that your children are physically and mentally healthy? Do you ever feel unhappy because they are behind their high-achieving friends?

4.4 Self-esteem versus self-worth

Often self-esteem and self-worth are mixed up and misunderstood. I will give two examples to Clarify between the two.

Imagine an ordinary person A is sitting in a Ford car while others are walking by; person A's self-esteem is high as other people walking by are wishing they had a car. Now another person B comes in a more luxurious car such as a BMW, Mercedes, or Audi and parks beside person A. Person B's self-esteem is very high, as person A wishes to have a luxury car like person B. Now another person C comes in a Ferrari or Lamborghini and parks next to person B. We know that person C's self-esteem is very high, but person B's self-esteem is low. This analogy can be seen as a very problematic situation. These three people are sitting in their cars, and their self-esteem depends on their cars and the cars they are parked next to; if they stop looking outside, stop comparing themselves with others and think about what they do have their perspective will change.

It is their self-worth. They may be driving an ordinary Ford car, but it is theirs. This cannot change. Now think about a helicopter crashing and seven people dying as a result. Now think about a helicopter crashing and seven people dying in it.

One was a world-renowned celebrity and six others were just 'normal' people. This crash and the celebrity will be mentioned in news across the world, and everyone will pay tributes and offer their condolences to the celebrity's family, but the other six will not be mentioned. The worth of these people is different in the eyes of the media and others, but if we go to the family of each of these seven people, they will each mourn their own family member. No one in the six people's families will be more upset about the celebrity than their own family member.

If we live in a house and create a new kitchen, we add to its value; when we fit new doors, we add to its value; when we install a new bathroom, we add to its value. Let us think of ourselves and our children like this: let us learn new skills, learn new languages and invest in something productive which will add value to ourselves and our personality, and increase our self-worth.

Every child goes to school and learns the same subjects. What are you doing differently to help your children stand out from the rest?

4.5 Bullying

Bullying is unwanted aggressive behaviour among school-aged children that involves a real or perceived power imbalance. The behaviour is repeated or has the potential to be repeated, over time.

There are three types of bullying:

Verbal bullying is saying or writing horrible things. It includes:

Teasing

Name-calling

Inappropriate sexual comments
Taunting
Threatening to cause harm.

Social bullying is sometimes referred to as relational bullying, and involves hurting someone's reputation or relationships. It includes:
Leaving someone out on purpose
Telling other children not to be friends with someone
Spreading rumours about someone
Embarrassing someone in public.

Physical bullying involves hurting a person's body or possessions. It includes:
Hitting/kicking/pinching
Spitting
Tripping/pushing
Taking or breaking someone's things
Making mean or rude hand gestures.

While conducting research for this book, I interviewed students under the age of 18 who were severely bullied at school, they stopped going to school and had to take their exams from home or went to special schools where the class-size was no more than four. Some of the students were tortured mentally on a daily basis to the point that they wanted to end their own lives. These students were perfectly normal, well-spoken, and intelligent, but some other students found it fun and entertaining to bully them and made them feel bad about themselves.

When children are bullied and victimised for their religion or the colour of their skin, they can become hesitant, uncomfortable or ashamed of their heritage and religion. We see some Muslims changing their names to non-Muslim names, just to avoid stereotypical behaviours towards them. Due to the negative portrayal of Muslims by the media, it is very easy and even normal to pick on Muslims, especially women and children as they are the most vulnerable and defenceless. This is rooted in racism and is a type of racism.

4.6 Islamophobia

This is rooted in racism and is a type of racism that targets expressions of Muslimness or perceived Muslimness.

Let us not allow some bullies to destroy our children's lives.

How can you support your children in these situations?

What do you know about bullying?

How do you deal with bullying yourself?

How do you help and support your children when they are being bullied?

How do you prepare and help your children when there is negative propaganda against Muslims in the media and in the general public?

Muslims in Europe

5.1 The concepts of halal and haram

As parents we look after our children and love them for who they are and what they do, but there are certain things which are forbidden in Islam, so we should stay clear about these rules and be firm with our children about them. These rules were created by Allah and it is in our children's best interest for us to steer our children away from the forbidden (haram) elements of life. Sometimes it may feel harsh, or our children may not like it, but these rules are absolute and we should obey them. If we take time and teach our children about halal and haram from an early age, it becomes easier for us and our children to obey these rules. However, if we neglect these rules and our children grow up with certain habits which are forbidden in Islam, it becomes very difficult to get rid of these habits. Habits are second nature and it is very difficult to change our nature.

Prophet Mohammad (P.B.U.H) said:

'Verily, the lawful (Halal) is clear and the unlawful (Haram) is clear, and between the two of them are doubtful matters about which many people do not know. Thus, he who avoids doubtful matters clears himself regarding his religion and his honour, and he who falls into doubtful matters will fall into the unlawful like the shepherd who pastures near a sanctuary, all but grazing therein. Verily, every king has a sanctum and the sanctum of Allah is his prohibitions. Verily, in the body is a piece of flesh which, if sound, the entire body is sound, and if corrupt, the entire body is corrupt. Truly, it is the heart.' [*Sahih Bukhari 52, Sahih Muslim 1599*]

Prophet Mohammad (P.B.U.H) divided the matters into three categories:

1. Halal (permissible)
2. Haram (not permissible)

3. And in between halal and haram, there are doubtful matters. Prophet Mohammad (P.B.U.H) advised Muslims to not fall in the doubtful matters, he said: 'So whoever abstains from the doubtful matters has saved his religion and his honour'.

The Quran has also clarified about what is forbidden to Muslims, Allah says in Surah Al-Baqarah, verse 172-173:

'O you who have believed, eat from the good things which We have provided for you and be grateful to Allah if it is [indeed] Him that you worship. He has only forbidden to you dead animals, blood, the flesh of swine, and that which has been dedicated to other than Allah. But whoever is forced [by necessity], neither desiring [it] nor transgressing [it's limit], there is no sin upon him. Indeed, Allah is Forgiving and Merciful'. [2:172-173]

It has been further explained in Surah Maidah, verse 3:

'Prohibited to you are dead animals, blood, the flesh of swine, and that which has been dedicated to other than Allah, and [those animals] killed by strangling or by a violent blow or by a head-long fall or by the goring of horns, and those from which a wild animal has eaten, except what you [are able to] slaughter [before its death], and those which are sacrificed on stone altars, and [prohibited is] that you seek decision through divining arrows. That is grave disobedience. This day those who disbelieve have despaired of [defeating] your religion; so fear them not, but fear Me. This day I have perfected for you your religion and completed My favour upon you and have approved for you Islam as religion. But whoever is forced by severe hunger with no inclination to sin - then indeed, Allah is Forgiving and Merciful'. [5:3]

What do you know about the commands of Allah concerning halal and haram?

How do you teach your children about halal and haram?

5.2 Parents who were born in other countries

Acknowledgment of the fact that you were born and raised in a different country, culture, and tradition, under very different parenting styles.

All those parents who were born in other countries will agree that our parents were very different: our fathers would be out earning money and our mothers would be housewives. We rarely saw our father having a conversation with our mothers or having a close relationship with her, but somehow, we were brought up in a stable household. There are several reasons behind this. One common reason was that we were brought up in big families and had many aunts and uncles; everyone knew us and what we were up to. If there was a problem, anyone could come and tell our parents, so we had to be very careful what we were doing.

Back home in our country, our parents would use a stick to discipline us and they could punish us for any wrongdoing, but fortunately or unfortunately, we cannot use those parenting styles in Europe to discipline our children. Here it is very straightforward: we reap what we sow. Here in Europe, family life is different, very different; everyone minds their own business and carries on with their own lives. If the parents are vigilant, they will keep an eye on what their children are doing. If they aren't, the children can do whatever they like. This is the main reason for the distance between family members: once children find a negative hobby and bad company, they spend most of their time there and their parents do not know a thing about it; whenever they do find out, it is too late. Again, when parents find out about their children's negative company and activities, instead of helping them, they fight with them and create a poisonous environment at home.

I always tell the parents during these parenting courses that it is impossible to live in the sea and remain dry. If we see Europe as a sea full of sins and we want our children to remain dry (free of sins), is it possible? Yes, if we have strong shoulders to carry them on until they can support themselves. It was our decision to come here to Europe, to have children and bring them up. We knew that he cultures and customs here are different, there is freedom to do anything and everything and a lot of things are over-sexualised. We still decided to bring up our children here. What were we expecting? That we would work every hour under the sun and that our children would grow up to be perfect Muslims miraculously?

It was reported that Umar bin al-Khattaab (RA) asked Ubay ibn Ka`ab (RA) about Taqwa. Ubay said, 'Have you ever walked on a path that has thorns on it?' Umar said, 'Yes.' Ubay said, 'What did you do then?' He said, 'I rolled up (my garment) and struggled (through the path).' Ubay said 'That is Taqwa.'

This Hadith was from 1400 years ago. Now think, we live in Western countries where almost everything is monetised and sexualised. There is sin at every step in our lives and there are opportunities for haram things on every corner. We are walking on a path full of thorns and shaitan is chasing and following us, but it is our decision to live here in the West, to have children and families here. Therefore, we have to deal with things, we cannot give up, we cannot hide from this challenge, and we cannot run away from it, as it is the reality of the time and place, we are living in. Imagine being a young Muslim in this situation, how difficult it is to refrain from committing sins, and to have the will to say no to haram things. Do we ever tell our children that when we were their age, we were so good, different, obedient, or grateful? Please do not say that to them ever again, as they are born and raised in a different country, culture, and environment from us.

Do we ever tell our children that when we were their age, we were so good, different, obedient, or grateful? Please do not say that to them ever again, as they are born and raised in a different country, culture, and environment from us.

5.3 The conflict of traditions and culture

You hold on to the traditions and culture of your parents. Do you expect your children to do the same, and why?

Are your children allowed to choose for themselves, and in what circumstances?

How much do you understand your children's mindset and circumstances?

5.4 Integration - to what extent?

Where is the limit or boundary in integration?

Some brothers and sisters live in Europe just as if they are living in their own countries, villages, or towns. They do not make any effort to learn the language or get used to local customs, while other brothers and sisters have changed their names, clothing, and appearances to fit in.

Which ones do you think is right, and why?

Do you think there is a middle ground, and if so, where is it?

Do you think you should respect the country and customs you are living in while not forgetting your own roots? In what way?

Your language, culture, and traditions (you, the parents) versus the language, culture, and way of life of your children where they are born and brought up

(Europe). Which of the following would you prioritise and emphasise for your children to follow?

Your mother tongue
Your culture and tradition
Your religion

Please write these in order, with reasons for each.

5.5 Identity

Asian, African, British, Asian-British, African-British, Muslim, British-Muslim. Let us be proud of who we are, where we came from and where we live in.

How do you identify yourself and what are your reasons for identifying that way?

How do you want your children to identify themselves and what reasons would you give them?

We have various identities, such as gender, caste, tribe, nationality, and religion. In which order do you identify yourself?

5.6 Concept of identity and crises of identity in Muslim youth

We Muslims are moving towards polarisation for various reasons, mainly because of negative media. For example, 'Islamists' or 'radical Muslims' are terms used for terrorists, and we Muslims like to dissociate ourselves from these terminologies. I still do not know what 'Islamist' means and who might identify as this, as it is a media-created term.

Secondly, we are always judged and put to the test to see if we are liberal or radical Muslims. We are judged by how we dress. We have to prove our Muslimness to Muslims if we are dressed in Western clothes and we have to prove our liberalness and moderation to non-Muslims if we are dressed in traditional or religious clothes. It is becoming difficult to express ourselves, our thoughts, and ways of dressing, which is a basic human right and a personal choice rather than a public rule.

I always believe in dressing however I like and I am comfortable in my clothes, regardless of what people think and say; it is my life and my choice, it is as simple as that.

On one occasion, I was travelling with my son, both of us dressed in our traditional clothes. We had to stop to do some shopping, but my son was hesitant about going into a supermarket dressed the way he was. We ended up having a good discussion in the car; I explained to my son, 'It is your life and your choice. As long as you don't hurt anyone, you should carry on with your lifestyle, ignoring what people may think or say.'

I gave my son an example, that once a man was travelling with his two children and his donkey. They were all walking and people said, 'Look, they have a donkey, but they are walking - how foolish they are!' So, they all climbed up onto the donkey and continued travelling. Then some other people said, 'Look, they are all riding on a poor donkey - how cruel they are!' So, the man climbed down while his children stayed on the donkey, and they continued travelling.

Next, some other people said, 'Look at that foolish man - he is walking himself while his children are riding on the donkey!' So he swapped position with his children.

Then some other people said, 'Look at that selfish man - he is riding on the donkey himself and his poor children are walking!' So the man picked up the donkey and they continued their journey.

Everyone laughed at them, saying, 'Look at these foolish people - instead of riding on the donkey, they have picked up the donkey!'

It did not matter how hard the man tried to please everyone, he still failed, and people ridiculed him.

It does not matter how we dress: people will still have an opinion about us, so let us ignore what people think or say, and just be true to ourselves and our religion. The only concern we should have is if we are pleasing Allah with our actions, lifestyle, and clothes or not; in the end, the only thing that matters is the pleasure or displeasure of Allah.

5.7 Protect your children!

How do you tell your children to avoid bad company (Muslim and non-Muslim)?

Narrated Abu Musa Al-Ash'ari (may Allah be pleased with him):

I heard Allah's Messenger (ﷺ) saying, 'The similitude of good company and that of bad company is that of the owner of musk and of the one blowing the bellows. The owner of musk would either offer you some free of charge, or you would buy it from him, or at least you would smell its pleasant odour; and as for the one who blows the bellows (i.e., the blacksmith), he would either burn your clothes or at least you shall have to smell a repugnant smell.' [*Al-Bukhari and Muslim*]

How well do you know your children's friends?

How well do you know where your children spend most of their time when they are outside?

5.8 Dealing with racism, bigotry, and stereotypical behaviour

We live in a country, society and time when we have to deal with ignorant people who tell us we do not belong here and we should go back to our countries. There are indeed racist and bigoted people, but we should not be affected by their ignorance and their opinions which are caused by their difficult and depressing lives.

It has become a pastime to talk about racism and bigotry all the time. I have seen this becoming a hobby, where we discuss and overthink what someone said about our skin colour, country, or religion. This creates negative energy, and we begin to judge everyone based on one remark by one person. If there is an opportunity to engage a person regarding racism, in dialogue, fine, but in most cases, these remarks are expressed by drunken people who are not in a position to engage in conversation. In this case, ignore the person and report them to authorities. I encourage everyone to do something about it, like engaging in productive dialogue or reporting it to the police. Just sitting down and dwelling on it does not help anyone; plus, this wastes our valuable time - we can do something productive with this time. Please let us not bring this home and dwell on it in front of our children, as children see everything in black and white and do not see the circumstances and complexities of the situation.

Most of us who came from other countries have different accents, habits and cultural influences (which is fine). people pick on these accents and habits. However, our children were born here, they speak the local language and have friends here, so we should accept the fact that our children's experiences may be different from ours; they may integrate better than us and may feel more patriotic than us. The point I am making is that it is our life, it is our family, it is our brain and we should not permanently accommodate negative people or negative behaviours. From now on, let us notice when we read a newspaper or watch the news, how a negative portrayal of people of colour changes our state of mind. The more we watch news about far-right terrorists, the angrier we get; if we do this every day, we will find ourselves angry every day. We can either limit watching news about far-right terrorists or develop a mechanism so that it will not ruin our day.

5.9 Safeguarding children from physical, mental, and sexual abuse

Remember, if we are not there for our children when they need help and support when they are upset, distressed and bullied, someone else will be. Our children will always remember these bad times - are we there for them?

Neglect	• Not meeting developmental milestones • Having poor hygiene • Lack of supervision i.e repeated and unexplained injuries • Appearing to care for family members • Tired, lack of energy and motivation
Physical abuse	• Broken bones • Scares • Fractures • Bite marks • Bruises • Burns • Scared and afraid of physical contact

Emotional abuse	• Being aggressive and cruel to other children and towards animals. • Lacking confidence and being anxious. • Lacking social skills. • Struggling to control emotions. • Withdrawal and isolation
Sexual abuse	• Appearing afraid to socialise or interact with a certain person • Avoiding being alone with certain people like family members or family friends • Anal or vaginal soreness. • The use of sexual language inappropriate for their age.

What to do if you notice any sign of abuse:

Open your eyes: If you open your eyes you will notice if they behaving differently, eat a lot more or less than they usually do and see if they have any unexplained cuts or bruises.

Open your arms and heart: If you notice any of these signs in your children show them love and affection and give them a sense of security. The best thing you can do for your children when they are distressed is to stay calm and give them an assurance that you will help, protect and support them.

Open your mouth: only Allah and you know how you feel and what your intention is. You need to listen to and speak to the people around you, you need to know what is going on in your family and what they are going through. This is only possible by open and free communication. In the majority of cases when children are abused, they hide it from their parents because of their pride, guilt and how their parents will react. If children know they will be supported by their parents they will always express their feelings and emotions openly.

Report: Report: Report: if and when you see any signs of any abuse report it to the teacher, the headteacher and local authority. Do not stop until you feel your child is safe. There are some parents who want their children to toughen up and deal with bullies and abuse even if it destroys their whole childhood. Sometimes some parents are labelled and shamed as overprotective, there is no such thing as overprotection if you feel your children will be harmed, bullied or abused – you should stand up for them. I hear this argument over and over that the world is a tough and merciless place but I always say I will make this world a beautiful place for my children until they are capable to make their own choices and deal with their own problems.

Until then their issues are my issues, their problems are my problems and I will never shy away from dealing with them. Report it to the school, local authority and police. The schools don't like it when they are reported to the police or the local authorities because they don't want to damage their reputation. It is unimportant for schools if your child is being bullied and your child has a traumatic livelihood, they are only concerned about not having a chain of abuse linked to their school as it damages their reputation.

5.10 What do we ask our children every day?

How was school? How was your day? Their answer is always 'Ok' or 'Fine.' Let us not feel embarrassed asking these questions below. We may feel and most certainly people around us will tell us that we are acting like British people. If something is right and it might help and protect our children, it does not matter where it comes from.

What can I do to help?	Who are the people you feel safe with?
Is there anything you want to talk about?	What makes you feel calm?
If you could change anything in your life, what it would be?	Where is a place you feel safe?
Is anyone upsetting you?	Is there anyone you are not comfortable with?
I am always there for you. You can tell me anything, even if you make a mistake.	What is your favourite and least favourite thing to do?

We need not bottle up all our feelings and emotions and keep them to ourselves. We can teach our children how to express their feelings and emotions. Mental health and well-being are as important as physical health. What are we doing about it, and what do we need to do about it? Start a conversation. Talk.

5.11 Internal racism and sectarian conflicts in Muslims

Unfortunately, we Muslims have certain perceptions and images about other Muslims of another colour and from other countries, races, or tribes. We make jokes about certain Muslims and discriminate against other Muslims because of their colour, country, or tribe. This is wrong and we always need to go back to the Quran and hadees for guidance.

Narrated Abu Musa (may Allah be pleased with him): The Prophet (ﷺ) said: 'A believer to another believer is like a building whose different parts Enforce each other'. The Prophet then clasped his hands with the fingers interlaced. [By Al Bukhari and Muslim]. The most honoured in the sight of Allah is the believer with the most Taqwa. The Glorious Quran illustrates this in Surah 49 Al Hujurat Verse 13:

يَا أَيُّهَا النَّاسُ إِنَّا خَلَقْنَاكُمْ مِنْ ذَكَرٍ وَأُنْثَىٰ وَجَعَلْنَاكُمْ شُعُوبًا وَقَبَائِلَ لِتَعَارَفُوا ۚ إِنَّ أَكْرَمَكُمْ عِنْدَ اللَّهِ أَتْقَاكُمْ ۚ إِنَّ اللَّهَ عَلِيمٌ خَبِيرٌ

'O mankind! We created you from a single (pair) of a male and a female, and made you into nations and tribes, that ye may know each other (not that ye may despise (each other). Verily the most honoured of you in the sight of Allah is (he who is) the most righteous of you (Muttaqi). And Allah has full knowledge and is well acquainted (with all things).'

It is not our gender, colour, country, tribe, lineage, or social status that means anything (or has any importance) in the sight of Allah, but with Allah it is Taqwa.

This problem exists when a young Muslim wants to marry a Muslim of another colour or from a different country or tribe. Muslims should stop this hypocrisy and follow the guidance of Allah and Prophet Muhammad.

What prejudices or perceptions do you have about Muslims of another colour or from other countries or tribes?

5.12 Happy parents - happy children - happy family

As we discussed in previous chapters, families work better together as one unit, since any part missing or not performing affects the whole family. So, what is the best way to bond together as a family?

The best way to start is to perform salah together in jummat at home. This action will bring everyone together, regardless of their age, role, position, or seniority within the family. Once we stand in front of Allah in one line, it will bring humility in our character. We all recognise and accept that Allah is the creator, the supreme power, and only he will guide us onto the right path. If you are reading this, my advice is to just do it, bring all your family together and start performing salah in jumaat. I do not know you and your family, but I can tell you that it will be a hard task to pray together. When we announce it and ask everyone to come for prayer, we are setting a high bar for ourselves. The first reason why this is difficult is that Shaitan will convince us not to do it, as we have to do it again and again, five times a day and it can be a hard task. The second reason is the fake egos of the older members of the family, as they will preach the whole day and night, but will hesitate to put their preaching into practice. A third reason is the distance between family members.

Some family members like to keep away from each other as far as possible, but if we want to be a family loved by Allah, if we want the help and protection of Allah, we have to start performing salah together. We can start with one prayer at a time when all the members of the family are home, free, and awake. I cannot explain in words how this one action will bring the whole family together and set an example for the little ones. We can preach to our children all day long, but can we turn our preaching into practice?

After performing salah, we should read one verse from the Quran and one hadees, and read the translation in any language we speak at home.

I can assure you from my personal experience and that of those who implemented this one action in their families: they have found peace and prosperity. It will only take ten minutes of your time. Please close your eyes and start this action without thinking.

You can read any verse from the Quran and hadees, and I have included short hadees for us parents to read to our children; they are easy and very relevant in our daily lives.

The Ultimate Success

6.1 Salah - prayer

Millions of people leave their families and countries of origin, and migrate to find a better future for themselves and their families. Some people put their lives in danger to enter countries where they believe they will find a better and successful life. Now, if you knew you can get a million pounds if you travel to another part of the country or another country, would you travel? If someone said you can get a million pounds if you relocate with your family, would you relocate? I think the answer will be yes, because people relocate for better careers and jobs. We relocate, leaving our countries, cities, friends, families, and children's schools, because we think it is for a better future and successful life. But when we hear Azaan five times a day, we hear the words:

'Hayya 'ala-s-Salah. Hayya 'ala-s-Salah.
Hayya 'ala-l-Falah. Hayya 'ala-l-Falah.'

In English, this translates as:

'Hurry to the prayer. Hurry to the prayer.
Hurry to salvation. Hurry to salvation.'

Five times a day, Allah says to us, Muslims, hurry to prayer and hurry to salvation, success, victory, and prosperity; we do not take it seriously, somehow, we do not believe it and cannot find time to grab this opportunity. We find time and energy to get ready for work, travel for work, and spend 10-12 hours working because we believe we will get a salary at the end of the month. We put so much effort and hard work into earning that money, but cannot find the time and energy to go to the mosque, or pray at home if there is no mosque nearby. The amazing thing is that a husband will force his wife to migrate to another country for few pounds, parents will drag their children across the globe to earn few pounds extra, but somehow that husband, wife, or parent cannot convince their partner or children to answer Allah's call and stand up for prayer. Here I will put forward a verse of the Quran and a hadees, without commentary as it is self-explanatory, for those who want to change and get closer to Allah.

Allah says in Quran:

'Indeed, those who recite the Book of Allah and establish prayer and spend [in His cause] out of what We have provided them, secretly and publicly, [can] expect a profit that will never perish' (*Quran, 35:29*).

Allah Almighty said in Holy Quran:

'And He will provide him from (sources) he never could imagine. And whosoever puts his trust in Allah, and then He will suffice him. Verily, Allah will accomplish his purpose. Indeed Allah has set a measure for all things' (*Surah Al-Talq, Verse 2-3*).

Abu Hurairah narrated that the Prophet (SAW) said,

'Allah says, O son of Adam! Take time out to constantly worship me, I will fill your heart with contentment, and remove your poverty, and if you do not do so. I will make your hands constantly occupied but I will not remove your poverty.' (*Tirmidhi*)

6.2 Hadees for children

`Umar Ibn Al-Khattâb (may Allah be pleased with him) said:

'I heard Allah's Messenger (ﷺ) saying: 'Deeds depend upon intentions and every person will get that which he intended. So whoever migrates for worldly benefits or for a woman to marry, his emigration will be for that which he migrated to.' (*Narrated by Al-Bukhaari and Muslim*)

It is reported on the authority of Ibn 'Umar (may Allah be pleased with him) that he said:

'Allaah's Messenger (ﷺ) said: 'Islaam is built upon five (pillars):
1. To testify that none is worthy of worship but Allaah and that Muhammad is the Messenger of Allaah.
2. To perform prayers.
3. To pay zakaah
4. (To perform) Hajj
5. To fast the month of Ramadhaan.' (Narrated by Al-Bukhaari and Muslim)

On the authority of 'Umar ibn Abi Salamah (may Allah be pleased with him), (it is reported that he said):

'I was a boy under the care of Allaah's Messenger (ﷺ) and my hand used to go around the dish; so Allaah's Messenger (ﷺ) said to me: 'Oh, boy! Mention the name of Allaah, eat with your right hand and eat from the dish what is nearest to you.' Since then, this has been my manner of eating.' (Narrated by Al-Bukhaari)

It is reported on the authority of Abu Qataadah (may Allah be pleased with him) that the Prophet (may Allah be pleased with him) said:

'A good dream is from Allaah and a bad dream is from Satan; so if any of you has a bad dream which makes him afraid, he should spit on his left side and he should seek refuge with Allaah from its evil, for then it will not harm him.' (Narrated by Al-Bukhaari)

Let us learn from our mistakes.

We can make mistakes. It is reported on the authority of Abu Hurairah (may Allah be pleased with him), from the Prophet (ﷺ) that he said:

'The Believer is not stung from the same hole twice.' (Narrated by Al-Bukhaari)

Greetings and charity.
Narrated Abdullah bin Amr (may Allah be pleased with him):

A man asked Allah's Messenger (ﷺ) 'Which act in Islam is the best?' The Prophet (ﷺ) replied 'To give food, and to greet those whom you know and those whom you do not know.' [*by Al-Bukhari&Muslim*] *Smile is good dead. Don't judge someone good dead if it is little*

Narrated Abu Dharr (may Allah be pleased with him):

Allah's Messenger (ﷺ) said: 'Do not disdain a good deed, (no matter how small it may seem) even if it is your meeting with your (Muslim)brother with a cheerful face.' [*Muslim*]

Best manners and character.
Abdullah bin Amr (may Allah be pleased with him) reported that the Prophet (ﷺ) was neither a fahish (one who speaks bad words) nor a mutafahish (one who speaks obscene evil words to make people laugh), He (ﷺ) never used bad language. He (ﷺ) used to say:

'The best amongst you are those who have the best manners and character'. [*by Al-Bukhari & Muslim*]

Do not be jealous of one another and do not cut ties.

Anas bin Malik (may Allah be pleased with him) narrated that Allah's messenger (ﷺ) said:

'Do not hate one another, and do not be jealous of one another, and do not desert each other, and O' Allah's worshippers! Be brothers. It is not permissible for any Muslim to desert (not talk to) his Muslim brother for more than three days'. [*Bukhari & Muslim*]

Do not harm others with your tongue and hands.
Abu Musa (may Allah be pleased with him) narrated that he asked Allah's Messenger (ﷺ):

Whose Islam is the best? (i.e. who is a good Muslim?). The Prophet (ﷺ) replied, 'One who avoids harming Muslims with his tongue and hands.' [*Al-Bukhari*]

Speak the truth.
Narrated Ibn Masaud (may Allah be pleased with him): Allah's Messenger (ﷺ) said: *'Truth leads to piety and piety leads to Paradise. A man persists in speaking the truth till he is recorded with Allah as a truthful man. Falsehood leads to transgression and transgression leads to Hell-fire. A man continues to speak falsehood till he is recorded*

with Allah as a great liar'. [*Al-Bukhari& Muslim*]

Internal racism based on caste, colour, or country.
Narrated Abu Musa (may Allah be pleased with him):

The Prophet (ﷺ) said: 'A believer to another believer is like a building whose different parts Enforce each other'. The Prophet then clasped his hands With the fingers interlaced. [*By Al Bukhari and Muslim*].

Narrated Abu Huraira (may Allah be pleased with him):

The Prophet (ﷺ) said 'The signs of a hypocrite are three:

1. Whenever he speaks, he tells a lie.
2. Whenever he promises, he always breaks it.
3. If you trust him, he proves to be dishonest (e.g. If you keep something as a trust with him, he will not return it). (*Al-Bukhari*)

Abu Juhaim (may Allah be pleased with him) said:

'Allaah's Messenger (ﷺ) said: 'If the person passing in front of a worshipper in prayer knew what a sin he was incurring, he would prefer to wait for forty (years) rather than passing in front of him.' (*Narrated by Al-Bukhaari*)

Narrated Abu Hurairah (may Allah be pleased with him):

Allah's Messenger (ﷺ) said: 'Do you know what backbiting is?' The companions said: 'Allah and His Messenger know better'. Thereupon he said, 'Backbiting is talking about your (Muslim) brother in a manner which he dislikes'. It was said to him: 'What if my (Muslim) brother is as I say. He (ﷺ) replied: 'If he is actually as you say, then that is backbiting; but if that is not in him, that is slandering.' [*Muslim*].

Narrated Abu Hurairah (may Allah be pleased with him):

Allah's Messenger (ﷺ) said: 'He who believes in Allah and the Last Day must not harm his neighbor; and he who believes in Allah and the Last Day must show hospitality to his guest; and he who believes in Allah and the Last Day must speak good or remain silent.' [*Al-Bukhari & Muslim*]

Narrated Abdullah ben Masud (may Allah be pleased with him):

Allah's Messenger (ﷺ) *said: 'He who has,in his heart, a grain of arrogance will not enter Paradise.' Someone said: How about a person who likes to wear beautiful clothes and shoes? Allah's Messenger* (ﷺ) *said 'All of Allah's Affairs are Beautiful and He likes beauty; arrogance means ridiculing and rejecting the Truth and despising people.'* [*Muslim*]

Narrated Abu Musa Al-Ash'ari (may Allah be pleased with him):

I *heard Allah's Messenger* (ﷺ) *saying, 'The similitude of good company and that of bad company is that of the owner of musk and of the one blowing the bellows. The owner of musk would either offer you some free of charge, or you would buy it from him, or at least you would smell its pleasant odour; and as for the one who blows the bellows(i.e., the blacksmith), he would either burn your clothes or at least you shall have to smell a repugnant smell.'* [*Al-Bukhari and Muslim*]

Narrated Abu Hurairah (may Allah be pleased with him) :

Allah's Messenger (ﷺ) *said: 'If anyone calls others to follow right guidance, his reward will be equivalent to those who follow him (in righteousness) without their reward being diminished in any respect on that account; and if anyone invites others to follow error, the sin, of which he is guilty, will be equivalent to those of the people who follow him (in sinfulness) without their sins being diminished in any respect on that account.'* [*Muslim*]

We should always work hard towards goodness and seek help from Allaah. We should always accept Allaah's Qadr.

It is reported on the authority of Abu Hurairah (may Allah be pleased with him) that Allaah's Messenger (ﷺ) said:

'The strong Believer is better and more loved by Allaah than the weak Believer, but in both of them there is good. Work hard for that which benefits you and seek help from Allaah and do not give up. If you are stricken by misfortune, do not say: 'If only

I had done such-and-such,' rather say: 'Allaah has decreed and what Allaah wills He does.' For verily, the words: 'If only...' Open the door to Satan's works.' (Narrated by Muslim).

People will judge you by your appearance and body, and Allah will judge you by your intentions and deeds. Do you put more effort into your appearance or deeds?

It is reported on the authority of Abu Hurairah (may Allah be pleased with him) that he said:

Allaah's Messenger (ﷺ) said: 'Verily, Allaah does not look at your bodies nor your appearance, but rather He looks at your hearts and your deeds.' (Narrated by Muslim)

Be kind to yourself, your family and people around you.

Protect yourself, your family and people around you.

References

https://www.bbc.co.uk/news/uk-31794599

https://www.independent.co.uk/news/uk/crime/muslims-jailed-drug-offences-surge-england-wales-prison-population-drop-a8259466.html

https://www.mentalhealth.org.uk/publications

https://www.nhs.uk/conditions/generalised-anxiety-disorder/

https://www.theguardian.com/society/2019/oct/15/hate-crimes-double-england-wales

What's Your Story? Young offenders' insights into tackling youth crime and its causes: User-Voice-Whats-Your-Story (http://www.uservoice.org/wp-content/uploads/2011/03/User-Voice-Whats-Your-Story.pdf)

https://www.theguardian.com/society/2015/jun/24/rise-proportion-black-ethnic-minority-young-prisoners-stop-and-search

https://www.theschoolrun.com/personal-hygiene-learning-children

https://docs.google.com/viewer?url=https://www.muslimlibrary.com/dl/books/30_Hadith_for_Children.pdf

https://www.muslim-library.com/english/30-hadiths-for-children/